IN THE LAB!

SCIENCE EXPERIMENTS FOR KIDS

Science and Nature for Kids

Speedy Publishing LLC
40 E. Main St. #1156
Newark, DE 19711
www.speedypublishing.com

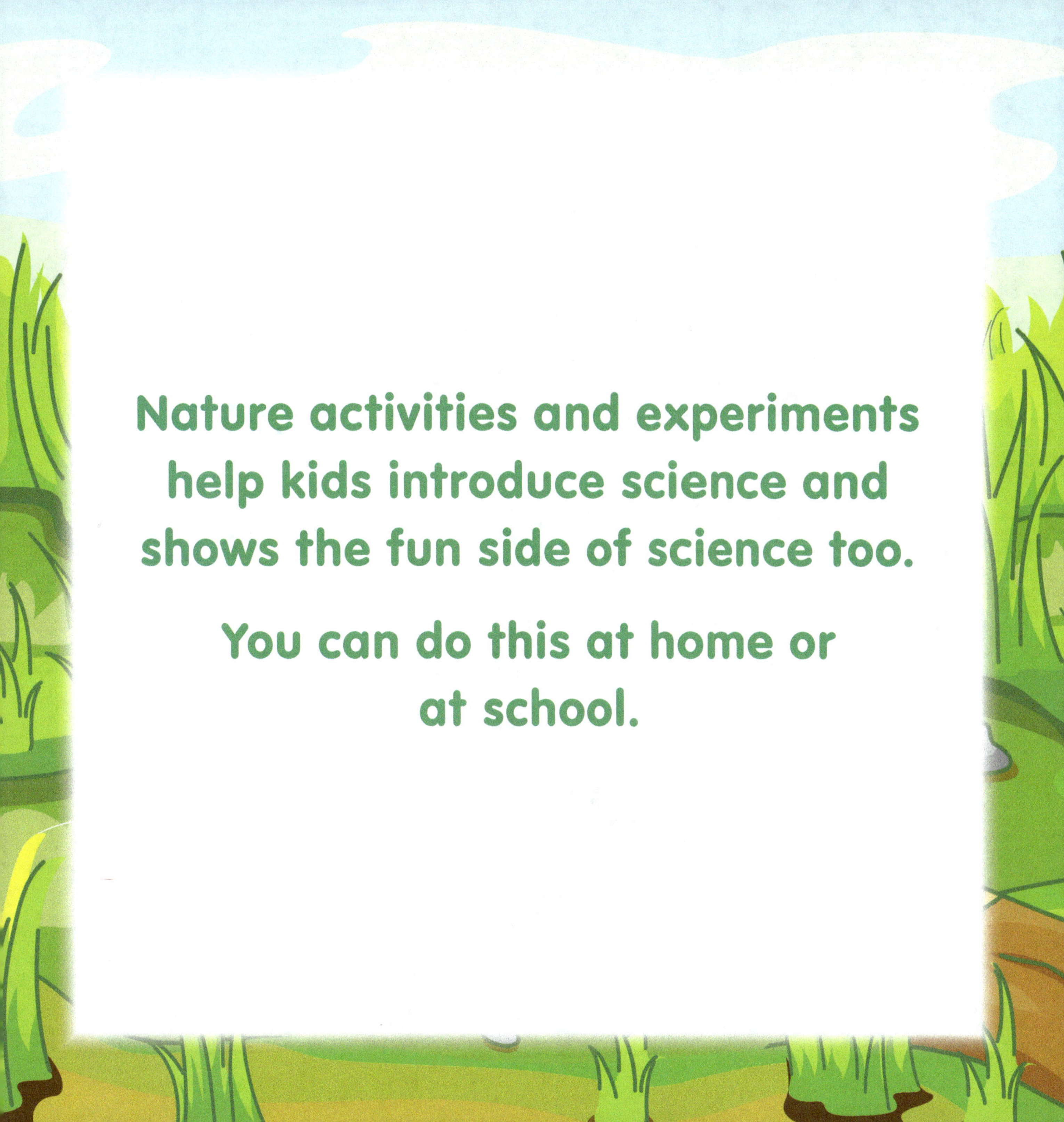

Nature activities and experiments help kids introduce science and shows the fun side of science too.

You can do this at home or at school.

SEE AND HAVE WITH THE FOLLOWING EXPERIMENTS

Rain in a Jar!

Make Your Own Rainbow

Do Plants Breathe?

Colorful Leafy Secrets

Where is Gravity?

RAIN IN A JAR

Call upon Mother Nature right inside your jar! Now you can enjoy rain whenever you wish.

This experiment also shows how is rain made.

THINGS YOU NEED

- Glass jar
- Plate
- Water
- Ice cubes

ACTIVITY

Boil water until you see it is steaming.
(please have an adult for supervision)

Fill 1/3rd of the glass jar with the steaming water.

Cover the mouth of the jar with a plate and wait for 2 minutes for the next step.

Place ice cubes on the plate and watch closely on what's happening inside the jar.

You can see there are little streams of water running down the surface of the jar just like the rain running down in the window.

WHAT'S GOING ON HERE?

When water becomes warm enough, it evaporates as vapor into the air. And when it cools the water vapor condenses and turns into tiny water droplets.

MAKE YOUR OWN RAINBOW

No need to wait for rain to see a real rainbow. This experiment will recreate the conditions which make rainbows appear, and teach you the science behind all those pretty colors while introducing the concept of refraction!

THINGS YOU NEED

- Sunny day
- Short drinking glass
- Sheet of white paper
- Water

ACTIVITY

Fill the glass about ¼ of the way full with water

Put the mirror in the glass

Then, turn the glass so the mirror faces the sun

Position the glass of water so that the sunlight shines on it

Hold the sheet of paper in front of the glass so that the rainbow can be easily seen.

The sunlight will pass through the water in the glass and refract (bend), forming many different colors on the surface of the sheet.

Hold the glass of water at different heights and angles while she watches for sunlight bouncing off the mirror.

WHAT'S GOING ON HERE?

The water in the glass bent the sunlight. When the light is bent, it breaks up into the different colors of the rainbow. This process is called refraction.

DO PLANTS BREATHE?

This experiment will show that plants are producing the oxygen we need to survive.

THINGS YOU NEED

- Zippered plastic bags
- A garden or place where there are different plants
- A nice sunny day

ACTIVITY

Find a variety of plants.

Try to select plants such as a vine, a shrub or tree and an herb or flower.

Remember, Do not pick the plant or remove any of its leaves, so choose something that you can slip a bag over without damaging the plant.

For the first plant, place your bag over the plant, or a portion of the plant, and zip the bag as far closed as possible without damaging the plant. You won't be able to close the bag completely, but that's okay.

Repeat Step 2 with other more plants.

Come back in 20 or 30 minutes.
What do you see? If you don't see anything, wait for another 20 or 30 minutes.

If you see water inside the bag they are droplets that have condensed. An evidence of the plants respiration process.

WHAT'S GOING ON HERE?

Plants take in carbon dioxide and give out oxygen, this process is called respiration.

It is the exchanging of two gases—oxygen and carbon dioxide to create energy in order to live.

COLORFUL LEAFY SECRETS

All leaves have hidden secrets!
This experiment will can unlock
the carefully hidden secret
colors of leaves.

THINGS YOU NEED

- Coffee filters
- Different kinds of leaves
- Isopropyl Alcohol
- Small glass jar with lids
- Droppers
- Small paper plates

ACTIVITY

Cut few leaves from one kind of tree into tiny pieces

Place leaf pieces in a glass jar and fill it with alcohol and replace the lid

Do the same thing for the other kinds of leaves

Leave the jars alone until the color of the alcohol turns green

Crease the filter strips to form a long V shape

Distribute a few drops of the alcohol from the jar to the filter strips (an inch from one end)

Let it dry

Pour half an inch of alcohol into a cup and put the filter strip into it

Cover the cup with a paper plate and wait for 15-20 minutes

Check the strips for bands of color

WHAT'S GOING ON HERE?

Leaves contain Chlorophyll. Chlorophyll makes the leaves green and it covers up all the other colors in the leaves. When it is exposed with alcohol the chlorophyll is washed away leaving the true color of the leaf.

WHERE IS GRAVITY?

This experiment is a fun way to demonstrate the concept of gravity. Observe how gravity is always pulling objects toward the Earth by using paperclips, magnets and other supplies.

THINGS YOU NEED

- Magnet
- Paper clip
- Thread or string
- Shoebox
- Scissors
- Tape

ACTIVITY

Take a small magnet and tape it to the insides of the shoebox to stand, the magnet should be at the top.

Tie a thread or string at the end of the paper clip
Hold the free end of the thread at the base of the shoebox.

Move the paper clip's end towards the top of the box.

Once it reaches the point where the paper clip can stay in air by itself, secure the free end of the thread to the base of the shoebox using a tape.

Observe the paper clip hanging by itself in midair.

WHAT'S GOING ON HERE?

Gravity is a force that tries to pull two objects toward each other.

Earth's gravity is what keeps us on the ground, what causes objects to fall, and is why the objects fall down rather than up!

There are more science experiments. Research and have fun!

Visit
BABY PROFESSOR
EDUCATION KIDS
www.BabyProfessorBooks.com
to download Free Baby Professor eBooks
and view our catalog of new and exciting
Children's Books

www.ingramcontent.com/pod-product-compliance
Lightning Source LLC
LaVergne TN
LVHW060831170826
845678LV00010B/1952

* 9 7 9 8 8 6 9 4 4 5 0 2 5 *